HOW TO GROW CARE MANAGE AND USE VIRGINIA STRAWBERRY FOR PROFIT

One Touch Guide On Cultivating, Nurturing, And Utilizing Virginia Strawberry For Financial Success

LARRY NANCY

"How to Grow, Care, Manage, and Use Virginia Strawberry for Profit" is a comprehensive guide that delves into the intricacies of cultivating Virginia strawberries, offering invaluable insights for both novice and experienced growers alike.

The book begins with an informative introduction in Chapter 1, providing readers with a foundational understanding of Virginia strawberries and their potential profitability.

Chapters 2 and 3 are devoted to the critical aspects of growing conditions and the planning and establishment of a strawberry farm. These sections guide farmers through the essential considerations, ensuring that they are well informed about the environmental requirements and strategic steps required for a successful venture.

Moving on to the practical components, Chapters 4 and 5 focus on planting, growing, and caring for Virginia strawberry plants.

The author includes practical suggestions and practices to maximize plant health and productivity, presenting a hands-on approach to crop management.

Chapter 6 emphasizes the importance of maximizing yield and quality, addressing methods to increase both the quantity and market value of the harvest, while Chapter 7 walks readers through post-harvest handling and storage techniques to ensure that the strawberries retain their freshness and appeal.

In Chapter 8, the book addresses the issues faced by pests and diseases, providing useful insights into successful management tactics. Chapter 9 focuses on financial management and profitability, providing growers with the knowledge needed to maintain a financially sustainable strawberry farm.

Finally, Chapter 10 broadens the horizon by exploring additional uses of Virginia strawberries, potentially unlocking new avenues of profit beyond traditional cultivation.

In essence, "How to Grow, Care, Manage, and Use Virginia Strawberry for Profit" is an indispensable resource, providing a holistic approach to strawberry farming that encompasses cultivation, care, profitability, and innovative applications.

CHAPTER ONE
AN INTRODUCTION TO VIRGINIA STRAWBERRIES

Virginia strawberries, scientifically known as Fragaria virginiana, have a rich history deeply embedded in the region's agricultural heritage. These succulent berries have been cultivated for centuries, contributing significantly to the agricultural landscape of Virginia. The state's unique climate and soil conditions provide an ideal environment for strawberry cultivation, making it a profitable venture for farmers.

The Rich History Of Virginia Strawberries

The history of Virginia strawberries is a fascinating journey that reflects the intersection of agricultural practices and cultural development. Native to North America, Virginia strawberries were cultivated by indigenous communities long before the arrival of European settlers.

Variety of Virginia Strawberries

Farmers can make informed decisions based on their farming goals and local climate if they are familiar with the various varieties of Virginia strawberries available. The 'Cavendish,' known for its sweetness, and the 'Chandl,' both of which have distinct characteristics such as size, flavor, disease resistance, and adaptability to particular growing conditions.

The Value Of Virginia Strawberries In Agriculture And Profitability

Virginia strawberries play a crucial role in both the agricultural sector and economic profitability. These berries, which are rich in vitamins, antioxidants, and other health-promoting compounds, are a sought-after commodity in the market. The demand for fresh, locally grown produce has increased, allowing farmers to capitalize on the popularity of Virginia strawberries.

Care And Management For Virginia Strawberries

2.1 Soil Preparation and Site Selection 2.2 Planting Techniques 2.3 Irrigation and Water Management 2.4 Fertilization Practices 2.5 Pest and Disease Management 2.6 Pruning and Run Control

Effective irrigation and water management are essential for preventing drought stress and ensuring consistent fruit development. Virginia strawberries thrive in well-drained, loamy soil with good sunlight exposure, so soil preparation and site selection are crucial. Planting techniques involve considerations such as proper spacing and depth to ensure optimal growth.

Pruning and runner control help to maintain plant vigor and promote the development of high-quality berries, while regular monitoring, early detection, and timely intervention are essential for preventing yield losses.

Farmers can optimize their Virginia strawberries by implementing these care and management practices.

Harvest and Post-Harvest Handling of Virginia Strawberries

3.1 Choosing the Best Harvest Time 3.2 Proper Harvesting Techniques 3.3 Post-Harvest Handling and Storage 3.4 Marketing Strategies for Fresh Virginia Strawberries 3.5 Value-Added Processing Opportunities

Proper harvesting techniques, such as using sharp tools and gentle handling, help maintain the fruit's quality, while post-harvest handling entails quick cooling and storage at optimal temperatures to extend shelf life and preserve freshness.

The optimal harvest time is crucial for achieving the desired level of ripeness and flavor.

Developing effective marketing strategies is critical for connecting with consumers and ensuring a profitable market presence for fresh Virginia strawberries. This may include establishing partnerships with local markets, participating in farmers' markets, or supplying to grocery stores. Additionally, exploring value-added processing opportunities, such as making jams, jellies, or frozen products, can diversify revenue streams and extend the market presence of Virginia strawberries.

Virginia strawberries are an important part of Virginia's agricultural landscape because of their historical significance, diverse varieties, and nutritional value. Farmers can maximize the yield and quality of their strawberries through careful care and management practices such as soil preparation, pest control, and proper harvesting techniques.

CHAPTER TWO
UNDERSTANDING THE GROWING CONDITIONS

Soil Requirements For Virginia Strawberries

Virginia strawberries thrive in well-drained, loamy soils with a slightly acidic to neutral pH ranging from 6.0 to 6.5. The soil should be rich in organic matter to foster robust root development and enhance nutrient availability. Adequate drainage is critical to prevent waterlogged conditions that may lead

Climate And Temperature Considerations:

Virginia strawberries thrive in temperate climates with cool winters and moderate summers, so understanding the specific temperature requirements is critical for successful farming. Ideally, the chilling requirement for strawberries should be met during the winter months, with temperatures ranging from 32°F to 45°F. Strawberries also require a certain

Sunlight And Watering Needs

Virginia strawberries thrive in full sunlight, requiring at least 6 to 8 hours of direct sunlight per day for optimal photosynthesis and fruit development. Poor fruiting and lower yields can result from an absence of enough sunshine. Consistent moisture levels are necessary for healthy growth, and drip irrigation systems are recommended.

Choosing The Ideal Location For Your Strawberry Farm

Choosing the right location is a strategic decision that significantly influences the overall success of a Virginia strawberry farm. The selected site should have well-drained soil, preferably elevated to prevent water stagnation, and a location with good air circulation helps mitigate the risk of fungal diseases.

Additionally, proximity to water sources for irrigation and ease of access for maintenance activities should be considered.

A thorough understanding of the growing conditions for Virginia strawberries is paramount for achieving success in commercial cultivation. This includes meticulous attention to soil quality, climate suitability, sunlight exposure, and water management, as well as strategic decision-making regarding the farm's location. By addressing these key factors, farmers can create an environment conducive to robust strawberry growth, eventually leading to increased yields and

CHAPTER THREE
PLANNING AND ESTABLISHING YOUR STRAWBERRY FARM
Developing A Comprehensive Business Plan

To be successful in strawberry farming, you must create a comprehensive business plan that outlines key aspects like goals, strategies, and financial projections. Begin by conducting thorough market research to identify consumer demand, competitors, and pricing trends, and clearly articulate your mission, vision, and objectives. The plan should also address potential challenges and risk mitigation strategies.

Sourcing Quality Strawberry Plants:

The success of a strawberry farm depends on the quality of the strawberry plants chosen for cultivation. It is imperative to source disease-resistant and high-yielding varieties suited to the local climate. Collaborating with reputable nurseries or certified suppliers ensures that the plants are free from pests and diseases, minimizing the risk of crop failure. Conduct thorough research on the specific cultivars that thrive in the Virginia region, taking factors such

Infrastructure and Layout Design for Maximum Growth:

The physical layout and infrastructure of a strawberry farm play a pivotal role in ensuring optimal growth and yield. Adequate planning should be devoted to designing efficient layouts for planting beds, irrigation systems, and protective structures such as tunnels or greenhouses. Consider the spacing between rows and plants, allowing for proper air circulation and sunlight exposure.

Economic and Financial Factors to Think About:

Creating a detailed budget that includes costs for land acquisition or lease, infrastructure setup, purchasing of quality planting material, labor, fertilizers, pesticides, and ongoing operational expenses is essential for successful strawberry farming. A contingency fund should be included in the budget to account for unexpected challenges.

CHAPTER FOUR
PLANTING AND CULTIVATING VIRGINIA STRAWBERRIES

Virginia strawberries, noted for their sweet flavor and brilliant red color, are a lucrative crop for anyone wishing to engage in profitable agriculture. Understanding and applying best practices throughout the planting phase is the key to cultivating Virginia strawberries successfully.

To ensure a strong start to your Virginia strawberry farm, it is critical to select high-quality plants from reputable nurseries. Choose disease-resistant varieties and inspect plants for any signs of pests or diseases before planting. The planting site should have well-drained soil with a slightly acidic pH ranging from 5.5 to 6.5. Proper soil preparation is paramount, involving thorough tilling and incorporation of

Proper row arrangement, such as using raised beds, aids in drainage and prevents waterlogging in a Virginia strawberry farm. Because strawberry plants require ample sunlight for optimal growth and fruit development, spacing should be designed to allow sunlight penetration and air circulation, thereby reducing the likelihood of fungal infections.

Mulching Techniques for Weed Control and Moisture Retention: Mulching is a key component in the cultivation of Virginia strawberries, offering multiple benefits for weed control and moisture retention. Applying a layer of organic mulch around the plants helps suppress weeds, reducing competition for nutrients and sunlight. This is especially crucial during the early stages of plant growth when strawberries are more vulnerable to weed interference.

A balanced fertilizer with a high phosphorus formulation is beneficial for promoting flower and fruit development; however, nitrogen application should be carefully managed to avoid excessive vegetative growth.

Regular soil testing is necessary to assess nutrient deficiencies and adjust fertilization practices accordingly.

Farmers can optimize yields, reduce disease risk, and cultivate a thriving and profitable strawberry enterprise by implementing best practices in planting and cultivating Virginia strawberries. These practices include careful consideration of planting techniques, spacing, mulching, and nutrient management.

CHAPTER FIVE
THE CARE AND MAINTENANCE OF VIRGINIA STRAWBERRY PLANTS

To prevent the spread of diseases like powdery mildew, verticillium, and powdery mildew, farmers must implement a comprehensive pest management strategy that includes the use of biological controls, organic pesticides, and careful inspection of the plants.

Pruning and training techniques are crucial for maximizing the yield of Virginia strawberry plants. Pruning involves the removal of dead or diseased plant material, as well as runners that divert energy away from fruit production.

Pruning improves air circulation, reduces disease risk, and promotes the development of large, high-quality berries. Training techniques, such as the use of trellises, help maintain an organized and efficient planting system.

Virginia strawberries thrive in well-drained soil with consistent moisture, and drip irrigation is a popular and efficient method for delivering water directly to the base of the plants while minimizing moisture on the leaves, thus reducing the risk of disease. Proper irrigation scheduling, taking into account the plant's growth stages, is also essential.

Farmers use row covers, frost blankets, and overhead irrigation to protect their strawberry plants from frost and cold, which can harm blossoms and young fruit, resulting in lower yields. Row covers act as insulators, trapping heat close to the plants and providing a shield against frost. Frost blankets, made of lightweight

The care and maintenance of Virginia strawberry plants necessitates a comprehensive approach that addresses pest and disease management, pruning and training techniques, irrigation systems, and frost protection strategies. Farmers who implement these practices can improve the overall health and productivity of their strawberry fields, resulting in a successful and profitable venture.

CHAPTER SIX
MAXIMIZING YIELD AND QUALITY

To maximize yield and quality in Virginia strawberry cultivation, it is critical to understand and manage various factors throughout the growth cycle. Successful cultivation begins with the selection of high-quality planting material, preferably disease-resistant varieties.

Adequate soil preparation is essential, focusing on well-drained, fertile soil with a slightly acidic pH. Regular monitoring of soil nutrient levels and pH, supplemented with appropriate fertilizers,

During the vegetative stage, proper care entails diligent weed control, irrigation management, and disease prevention measures. A well-designed irrigation system helps maintain soil moisture at an optimal level, preventing water stress that could negatively impact plant development. Integrated pest management practices should be implemented to address potential threats without jeopardizing crop health.

1. Flower and Fruit Development Stages:

Understanding the flower and fruit development stages is critical for effective management.

The flowering stage, which marks the transition from vegetative growth to reproductive development, requires careful attention to environmental conditions, particularly temperature and light, to facilitate successful pollination. Understanding the various flower types and their role in fruit development aids in identifying potential issues and implementing corrective actions.

Proper management during the critical stages of fruit development, such as fertilization, seed formation, and fruit maturation, has a significant impact on the overall yield and quality of Virginia strawberries. By monitoring these stages, timely interventions like adjusting nutrient application and irrigation regimes can be made.

2 Pollination Techniques for Higher Yield:

While Virginia strawberries are primarily self-pollinating, introducing pollinators like honeybees can significantly increase yields. Creating a favorable environment for pollinators entails maintaining diverse floral resources, minimizing pesticide use, and providing nesting sites.

Adopting a holistic approach to pollination management contributes to increased fruit set, resulting in higher yields. Techniques such as hive placement and strategic planting layouts can be used to optimize pollination efficiency, and monitoring weather conditions and aligning pollination activities with favorable periods further improves its effectiveness.

3 Thinning Techniques for Larger, Sweeter Berries:

Thinning, which involves removing excess fruits to redirect the plant's resources towards fewer, high-quality berries, plays a pivotal role in ensuring larger and sweeter berries.

This process prevents overcrowding and facilitates better air circulation, reducing the risk of diseases. Thinning should begin in the early stages of fruit development, targeting clusters with smaller or misshapen berries.

To achieve the desired fruit quality, it is critical to strike the right balance between the number of berries and the plant's ability to support their growth. The thinning process is guided by careful consideration of plant vigor, fruit size distribution, and overall plant health. Thinning practices promote uniform fruit size, increase sweetness, and make harvesting easier.

4. Harvesting at the Peak of Ripeness

Harvesting Virginia strawberries at the peak of ripeness is critical for maximizing flavor, aroma, and overall quality. Regular monitoring of fruit color, size, and taste aids in determining the optimal harvest time. Harvesting too early can result in underripe berries that lack sweetness and flavor while harvesting too late can result in overripe fruit with diminished quality.

The marketability and profitability of Virginia strawberry cultivation are significantly impacted by timely and meticulous harvesting practices. Using sharp, clean tools and handling berries with care minimizes damage and ensures post-harvest longevity, while a staggered harvesting approach ensures a continuous supply of fresh berries to meet market demands.

CHAPTER SEVEN
POST-HARVEST HANDLING AND STORAGE

Best Practices for Harvesting Virginia Strawberries:

Efficient harvesting is a critical factor in maximizing the quality and yield of Virginia strawberries. Typically, strawberries are picked when they reach full color and have a firm texture. It is crucial to handle the berries gently to minimize bruising and damage. Harvesting during cool periods of the day, such as early morning or late evening, helps preserve the quality of the fruit.

<u>Immediate Postharvest Handling Techniques:</u>

To preserve the freshness and quality of Virginia strawberries, they must be handled immediately after harvest. To slow down the ripening process and prevent decay, pre-cooling methods like hydrocooling or forced-air cooling are commonly used to rapidly lower the temperature of the strawberries. Sorting and grading are necessary steps to remove damaged or overripe berries and ensure that only the

<u>Storage Options for Maintaining Freshness:</u>

Controlled atmosphere storage, which adjusts oxygen and carbon dioxide levels, can extend the shelf life of Virginia strawberries and keep them fresh for commercial purposes. Cold storage facilities with controlled humidity and temperature are ideal for preserving the berries. Refrigeration temperatures around 32°F (0°C) are appropriate for strawberries, preventing decay while minimizing moisture loss.

<u>Packaging and Marketing Strategy:</u>

Strawberry packaging, such as clamshell containers, breathable plastic bags, or vented cartons, should be designed to protect the berries during transportation while also allowing for proper ventilation to prevent moisture buildup.

Labeling should include essential information like the variety, origin, and handling instructions.

CHAPTER EIGHT
CONTROLLING INSECTS AND DISEASES

Virginia strawberry cultivation, like any other agricultural endeavor, faces challenges from pests and diseases that can potentially jeopardize yields and profitability. To effectively manage these threats, growers must be adept at identifying common pests and implementing appropriate control measures. Understanding the lifecycle, behavior, and appearance of pests specific to Virginia strawberries is paramount.

Identifying Common Pests of Virginia Strawberries:

Aphids, tiny insects that feed on plant sap, can quickly multiply and cause stunted growth in strawberry plants. Spider mites, on on the flip side, are spiders that do harm viapiercing plant cells and extracting nutrients, resulting in yellowed leaves and reduced photosynthesis. Strawberry root weevils can cause severe da

<u>Organic and Chemical Pest Control Techniques:</u>

To maintain healthy strawberry crops, effective pest control methods are crucial. Organic approaches involve the use of natural predators, such as ladybugs and predatory mites, to control aphid and spider mite populations. Additionally, neem oil and insecticidal soaps derived from natural sources can be used as organic alternatives. Chemical pest control involves the use of synthetic pesticides, but careful consideration must be given to potential

<u>Approaches to Health Promotion and Disease Management:</u>

Botrytis cinerea, the gray mold, and Colletotrichum spp., the anthracnose, are two common diseases that threaten Virginia strawberries. Gray mold, which thrives in cool and humid conditions, causes fuzzy gray lesions on fruit, compromising both quality and marketability.

Anthracnose, which causes dark lesions on berries, stems, and leaves, thrives in warm and wet conditions. Taking preventive measures, such as proper plant spacing, adequate

<u>Integrated Pest Management in Sustainable Farming:</u>

Integrated Pest Management (IPM), which combines biological, cultural, and chemical control methods to manage pests and diseases in an environmentally conscious manner, is essential for sustainable strawberry farming in Virginia. Growers can reduce their reliance on chemical interventions by incorporating pest-resistant varieties, practicing crop rotation, and promoting natural predators. Regular monitoring and early detection play key roles in the success of

CHAPTER NINE
FINANCIAL MANAGEMENT AND PROFITABILITY

Cost analysis and budgeting are critical components of successful Virginia strawberry farming for profit. To maximize returns, farmers must meticulously examine all incurred expenses associated with cultivating and managing the strawberry crops, including costs related to land preparation, seedlings, fertilizers, pesticides, irrigation, labor, and equipment.

Pricing Strategies for Profitable Sales: Developing effective pricing strategies is paramount for ensuring profitability in the Virginia strawberry farming business. Farmers need to consider various factors when determining the prices of their strawberries, such as production costs, market demand, competition, and quality. Striking a balance between offering competitive prices and covering production costs is essential.

Furthermore, understanding market dynamics and con

Creating and marketing value-added products, such as strawberry jams, jellies, sauces, or even incorporating strawberries into baked goods, can significantly increase the profitability of Virginia strawberry farming operations by diversifying revenue streams.

Maintaining accurate and detailed records is a fundamental aspect of sound financial management in Virginia strawberry farming.

This includes documentation of expenses, revenues, crop yields, and market trends.

These records facilitate informed decision-making, allowing farmers to identify areas of improvement, assess the effectiveness of various strategies, and make adjustments accordingly. Advanced record-keeping systems, often

CHAPTER TEN
EXPLORING ADDITIONAL USES FOR VIRGINIA STRAWBERRIES

Virginia strawberries, in addition to their intrinsic appeal as a delectable fruit, present a myriad of opportunities for culinary applications. Restaurants, bakeries, and catering services can capitalize on the unique flavor profile of Virginia strawberries, incorporating them into diverse dishes.

Chefs can experiment with incorporating the berries into salads, desserts, and even savory dishes, creating a niche market for culinary delights.

Furthermore, exploring the creation of value-added products opens up new avenues for profit. Jams, jellies, and fruit preserves crafted from Virginia strawberries provide an excellent means of extending the shelf life of the fruit and catering to consumers looking for convenient, ready-to-use products.

Virginia strawberry growers can diversify their income streams by exploring direct-to-consumer models such as farmers' markets, subscription boxes, or community-supported agriculture (CSA) programs.

Collaborating with local businesses, such as ice cream shops, bakeries, or artisanal food producers, can lead to mutually beneficial partnerships that enhance the brand.

Cooperative efforts within the agricultural community, such as forming alliances with them, can increase the reach of Virginia strawberries and create a buzz around their distinctive qualities.

Partnerships with grocery stores, supermarkets, or specialty food stores can secure consistent distribution channels, ensuring a steady income stream.

CONCLUSION

The cultivation of Virginia strawberries offers not only a flavorful fruit but also a path to sustainable and profitable agricultural endeavors.

Effective cultivation practices, such as selecting suitable varieties, implementing proper soil management, and employing pest control measures, lay the foundation for a successful harvest. Rigorous care, including irrigation, fertilization, and disease prevention, ensures the health and vitality of the strawberry plants.

Furthermore, strategic management involves crop rotation, pest monitoring, and adapting cultivation practices to the local climate, contributing to the long-term viability of the strawberry farm.

Using sustainable and eco-friendly practices not only aligns with modern agricultural trends but also safeguards the environment for future generations. Integrating technological advancements, such as precision farming and automated irrigation systems, enhances efficiency and

Beyond the cultivation phase, effective marketing strategies are crucial for maximizing profitability. Understanding the target market, leveraging online platforms, and utilizing social media can amplify the visibility of Virginia strawberries. Exploring niche markets, such as organic or locally sourced produce, can open up premium pricing opportunities. Furthermore, participating in farmers' markets, agricultural fairs, and community events fosters direct connections with

Collaboration and partnerships with local businesses and agricultural communities pave the way for sustained growth and market expansion. The comprehensive approach outlined here, from cultivation to marketing and product diversification, provides a holistic guide for harnessing the potential of Virginia strawberries.